Secrets
After
Birth

By Evelyn Quinn

Dedicated to all those mothers who struggled in silence, cried in solitude, and wished they knew they weren't alone...

Welcome

We're here to talk about the stuff that happens after childbirth — the embarrassing, the awkward, and the downright confusing. It's about sharing the essentials, the unglamorous, and the everyday experiences that no one talks about, but every new mum faces.

This is everything I wish my midwife had told me...

Yours,
Evelyn

Secrets After Birth

My mission is simple: to share the unspoken side of postpartum life. No sugar-coating, no fluff – just real stories, real struggles, and real laughs. This isn't professional advice; it's a collection of honest tales and insights from the post-birth trenches, aimed at helping other mums feel less alone and more understood in their own journeys.

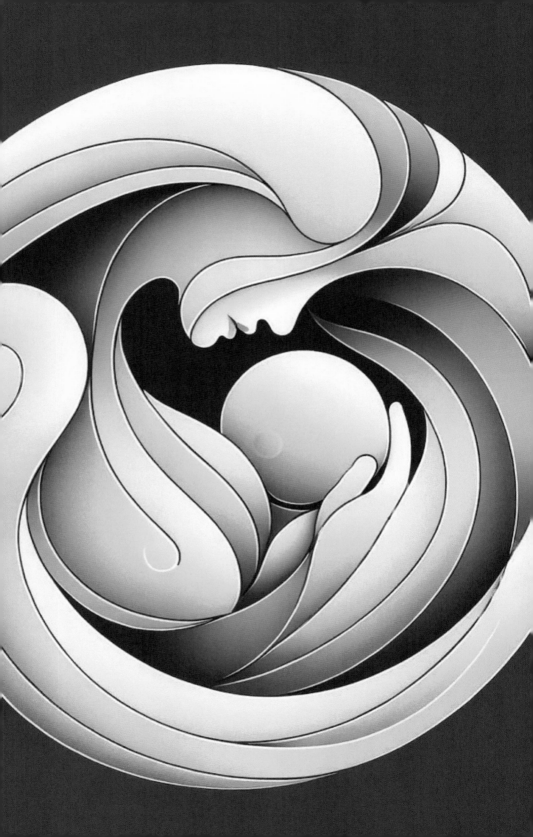

Secrets After Birth

Your Journey:

First two weeks

*

Next six weeks

*

Breastfeeding

*

Partner's Playbook

*

First two weeks

Postpartum Chronicles:
The Real Deal on Tears, Pads, and Night Sweats

A blur of nappies, night feeds, and realising that hot tea is now a thing of myths and legends.

Let's be honest; it's a roller-coaster ride like no other. Those first two weeks postpartum? Brace yourself because you're in for a wild and emotional adventure. From tears to pads and everything in between, here's what nobody really tells you about navigating those crucial initial days.

First two weeks

The Tearful Beginning

So there I was, post-birth, a bundle of emotions, and I couldn't tell my birth story without the waterworks. Picture this: a tsunami of tears, and I'm not talking about those happy ones you see in the movies. Nope, these were the kind fuelled by pregnancy hormones packing their bags and new milk-making hormones taking their place. Get ready, mama, for an emotional roller-coaster of epic proportions. It's like an emotional hurricane, and you're in the eye of the storm. But guess what? It's perfectly normal. Embrace the tears; they're part of the beautiful chaos of motherhood.

The Battle of the Pads

Let's get practical. Maternity pads are your new best friends, and you'll need an army of them—about 70. During those first few days, you'll be changing them 10x a day. Here's a secret weapon: slather some aloe vera on those pads and chill them in the fridge. Trust me; this icy coolness is a game-changer. After 10 days you can move to normal period pads. No tampons! I stopped bleeding after a month.

First two weeks

The Healing 5-5-5

Your body is an incredible powerhouse, but it still needs time to heal. The first few weeks postpartum are all about recovery. Think 5-5-5: 5 days in the bed, 5 days on the bed, 5 days near the bed. You may still experience some discomfort, bleeding, and pelvic floor challenges. Don't be surprised if you occasionally feel like a marathon runner who just finished a race. Rest assured, it gets better. It is important you have a postpartum checkup at the doctors. I had to beg for one from my GP and it was humiliating. It is not routine across the UK to have a checkup after birth. How crazy is that? Your whole body goes through extreme trauma and you're lucky if you get a cuppa on the way out the door of the delivery room!

First two weeks

The Loo Challenge

Control over your bladder? Every time you think you might need the loo, don't hesitate – make a beeline for it. Those pelvic muscles are exhausted; they need some time to regain their strength. So, heed the call of nature, and don't hold back. This is especially true if you had an epidural and therefore also had a catheter (a tube that is inserted into your bladder, allowing your urine to drain freely). It was day two after giving birth. My baby needed a nappy change. I was standing there over the changing table, trying to move as quickly as possible. I started to do the classic pee dance; I was holding as much as I could but it didn't matter. I felt a trickle down my leg. I was mortified. In unison, tears trickled down my cheeks. I now look back and know I should have just given the baby to my husband or shouted for him to come through, but I didn't want to disturb him. This mindset of trying to do it myself and not wanting to bother my husband was the wrong mindset. Your partner should be the one changing nappies while you are resting your sleep-deprived pelvic floor!

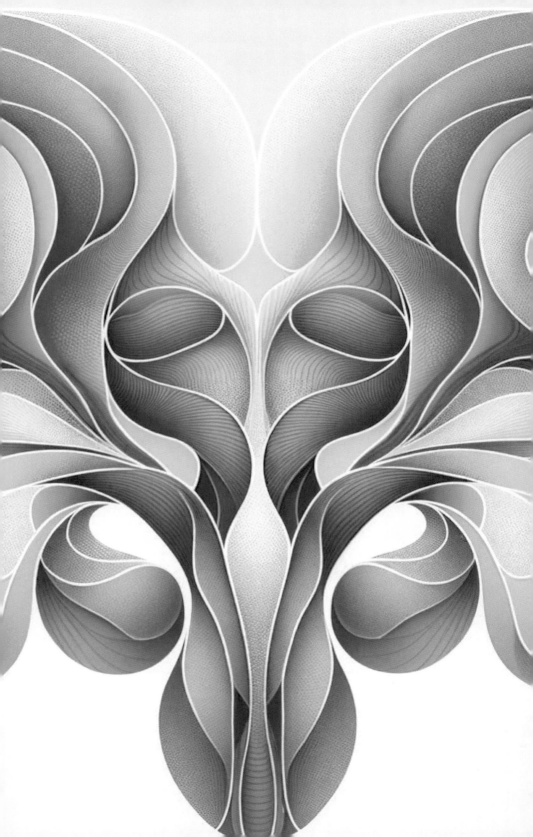

First two weeks

Mama Takes the Lead

Here's a truth bomb: Mama is the real MVP in the house, not the baby. I know it sounds counter-intuitive, but hear me out. Your little one's top priority is a happy and healthy mum. So, it's not just okay but essential to put your needs first. You need to be your best self to take care of your baby, and that starts with self-care. Guilt-free self-care. You need to talk to your partner about this and in our sister book, 'Parenthood Pledge' I guide you through that conversation.

Feeding Messiness

As your milk supply kicks into high gear, your baby might become a messy feeder. This means you'll want to feed on a towel in bed to avoid falling asleep on a wet patch. Trust me; it's a small but mighty life hack. Muslims in every room and handbag are a huge help too.

First two weeks

Daily Dettol Ritual

Daily Dettol baths? Yep, they're a thing, and they're about as glamorous as they sound. This isn't your spa day; it's about disinfection. Keeping things clean and fresh down there is crucial for your postpartum recovery. I had an episiotomy. It took Dr Omar 1.5 hours to sew me back together. At one stage, I looked down between my legs and joked, 'making me look as good as new down there?' Dr Omar stared into the abyss and replied, 'I wouldn't say that, no'. Dettol baths ensured I did not get infected. I did them for a month. No bubble bath or anything else. Your partner should ensure they schedule time to look after the baby, so you have time to do this.

First two weeks

Baby Handful

A newborn baby will want to be held as much as possible. As wonderful as this sounds it makes it hard to achieve anything other than holding the baby and until the baby can hold their own head up (3 months ish), then you will be using two hands. I thought that after I gave birth I would get an element of autonomy over my body back. But that's not true for quite a while longer. And trips away? Some parents can leave their baby overnight as early as 3 months. Some go away for a week at 6 months. I left my baby for 36 hours at 7 months and it was too early. She refused to eat or take the bottle. I shouldn't have left her. There is no right time frame, so plan to be with your baby as long as possible and only plan a trip away once you know they are ready.

First two weeks

Sleep Deprivation

What you might not expect is that the baby will sleep fairly well the first night. They are literally exhausted from their own birth. You make wake in a panic rushing to their side to check they are breathing, but no need to worry. They will wake you when they need a feed and while the first night is not as bad as expected, the second night is worse. Waking every hour to feed is no easy shift. It's utterly draining. I wish I could say something helpful about sleep, but some babies don't sleep for a long time. I read all the books, I tried all the tricks. It is more about the baby than the technique so if yours isn't a sleeper, know you're not alone. And the only reassuring thing I can say is that while it's tough, your body learns to cope much better than you'd ever expect. When it feels too tough, your partner must step in to help during the night. Even if you are breastfeeding. They can burp and change the baby. You could consider a night nurse, but for most people, it's cost-prohibitive (£200pn) and you never know when your baby will have a good night. Even on bad nights, you'll still be up breastfeeding so it's a high price for medium support. Someone allowing you to sleep in the morning may be more beneficial.

First two weeks

The Night Sweats Surprise
Here's something nobody told me: night sweats can start at 1-2 weeks postpartum. It's like your body's way of saying goodbye to those pregnancy hormones. To cope, lie on a towel in bed, and be prepared for about 10 days of waking up drenched. If your partner wants brownie points then they should wash your pillow case regularly during this time.

Embracing the Chaos
So, there you have it – the raw, real, and unfiltered truth about the first two weeks postpartum. It's a time of tears, pads, and unexpected surprises, but it's also a time of profound love and resilience. Remember, you're not alone on this journey, and the chaos is all part of the beautiful tapestry of motherhood. Embrace it, treasure it, and know that you're doing an incredible job. Welcome to the wonderful world of parenthood!

Next six weeks

First two months: Who cried more? You or the baby?

This period is a continuation of the roller-coaster ride you started in those first two weeks, but trust me, it's a journey filled with its own unique challenges and surprises. From healing to baby bonding and a *dash* of sleep deprivation, here's what to expect as you navigate this pivotal phase of early motherhood.

Next six weeks

Nourishing Nutrition

Healing post-birth is an art and your palette? Nutrition. Think of protein and collagen as your best friends for recovery. After childbirth, and while you're busy producing that liquid gold called breast milk, your estrogen levels take a bit of a holiday. Now, estrogen is like the fairy godmother of collagen production, essential for repairing tissues and muscles. But with your body on a bit of an estrogen break, it's time to call in reinforcements through your diet. Stock up on foods rich in these nutrients to help your body recover! I took beef bone broth and liquid collagen to support my recovery.

Hair Horror

Something I didn't know, your hair can change after birth, not only does it thin, but it can go curly or change colour. My natural blonde went dark and I thought someone else was in my house when I found strands all over the place! I actually asked my husband, rather curtly, 'who's hair is this?' Whoops! Nutrition can help minimise this.

Next six weeks

Pelvic Floor

Getting on the path to recovery six weeks postpartum could change your life. Please don't underestimate the struggles of a weak pelvic floor. Think peeing a little while sneezing, coughing, or laughing. Or even worse, a prolapse.

To strengthen your pelvic floor, it's important to practice Kegel exercises, physiotherapy, and potentially include Pilates. The NHS 'Squeezy' app is a surprisingly good tool. Consider a private 'mummy MOT' if needed, which costs around £100-200; it's a worthwhile investment for your postpartum recovery and long-term well-being.

Starting pelvic floor exercises during pregnancy is beneficial. Integrating them into your routine, such as during breastfeeding sessions, ensures consistency. To perform a Kegel exercise, sit with feet flat or lie down with uncrossed legs. Inhale and relax, then exhale while contracting your muscles from the back passage to the front, as if holding in a fart and then a wee. Imagine pulling up a piece of spaghetti into your hoo-hoo! Do this 10x and then do 10x quick squeeze and release.

Next six weeks

Prolapse

If you are like me, you may never have heard of a prolapse. It is mad that this is fairly common after birth and midwives or doctors don't tell you about it! There can be several different types of prolapse - anterior, uterine, and posterior. It feels like a bulge. It was 10pm, I had just put my baby down who had been screaming in colicky pain for 6 hours. I knew something was wrong. I went to the bathroom and looked in the mirror for the first time since birth. I didn't know what I was looking at but I knew it wasn't right. I started to panic. I then made the worst decision, I googled it. Google told me it was a uterine prolapse and I may need a hysterectomy. I was scared and devastated. I went back to bed and wept silently next to my baby. I'm not telling you this to scare you. I'm telling you because if you rest and focus on nutrition and self-care, then you will fully recover. But if you jump to your feet and try to live life like it was before or try to be a super mum by doing it all yourself, then chances are you will have a postpartum complication. I had an anterior prolapse. It took longer than expected to recover (18 months) and a huge commitment to physio and Pilates. My husband couldn't tell, it was an internal feeling of discomfort.

Next six weeks

Post-birth complications (continued)

Other complications include your stitches getting infected, and there are a multitude of other issues. These risks should not be secrets! Your midwife should have told you. But in lieu of that, I beg you to rest and recover! You will be so much happier. If you do develop any post-birth complications. Don't worry. Don't be afraid, like I was. You will recover, it will just take longer. You will feel like yourself again, but you will need patience and support, potentially from a physiotherapist. Recovery should become part of your daily routine. You can do some of this in bed. A gentle but powerful recovery move is to lie on your back, feet flat on the floor/bed, knees bent and hip-width apart. Deep inhale, on the exhale, engage the pelvic floor and lift your head and shoulders, pause at the top, inhale on your return down. This won't be suitable for anyone with a C-Section.

Next six weeks

Ab Separation

After childbirth, many new mothers discover they have diastasis recti, where the abdominal muscles have separated more than usual. It's a common but often unexpected part of postpartum recovery. You can tell during pregnancy because if you lean back, there is a cone-shaped raise between your abs. If you find yourself in this situation, know that it's a normal occurrence and you're not alone. Recovery involves specific exercises and a fair amount of patience. It's important to be kind to yourself during this time and to seek guidance from healthcare professionals who can provide tailored advice and support. Breathing correctly during your exercises is absolutely key. Similar to the pelvic floor, where you exhale while engaging the muscles, if you use breathing during your ab recovery you will recover faster and better. Some people do not know they have diastasis recti and they think can't lose weight around the belly, but actually it's because your ab muscles are not holding in your internal organs. Do not just hit the gym like you did before! You need specialised exercises to draw the abs back together.

Next six weeks

Colic

I had read about Colic. I was determined that my baby would not have it. I would do everything right. The 5 S's (swaddling, side or stomach position, shushing, swinging, and sucking); getting the temperature right; sleep windows; etc. It didn't matter. By week two we knew she had colic. It didn't leave us until 3-4 months and then when we tried to move to solids at 6 months it is as though it returned. It was hell. Worse than I could imagine. It started around 3pm and lasted 6 hours. During this time she screamed nonstop. She had a stiff arched back, stiff legs, eyes to the ceiling. She was in agonising pain. It was so awful to experience, watching her in pain and knowing I couldn't help. I tried gripe water and colic drops. Nothing helped. Her face would be bright red. You had to hold her for these 6 hours and be bobbing and swaying, trying to help. Doctors or health care workers didn't help, I was told, condescendingly, 'you're just struggling as a first-time mum'. I tried an osteopath, but no luck either. Her colic was the hardest time in my life. It is utterly heartbreaking and exhausting. I don't have a magic cure for you, but know you're not alone and seek help from family, friends and doctors to give yourself respite.

Next six weeks

A Different Kind of Emotional Roller-coaster

The emotional roller-coaster isn't over; it's just taking a new twist. You might find yourself experiencing a whirlwind of feelings – from pure joy at gazing into your baby's eyes to moments of doubt and exhaustion. It's all part of the process, and it's okay to not have it all figured out. It's not unusual for new mothers to experience thoughts that can be pretty scary. In the whirlwind of postpartum emotions, your mind can sometimes conjure up vivid and alarming scenarios. I often imagined tripping down the stairs while carrying my baby and one or both of us breaking our necks. These thoughts can be distressing, but they're more common than you might think. It's essential to remember that these are just thoughts – your brain's way of processing the immense responsibility and love that come with motherhood. If these thoughts become overwhelming or cause you significant distress, don't hesitate to reach out to a healthcare professional or a support network. You're not alone, and seeking help is a sign of strength and love for your little one.

Next six weeks

Sleep Deprivation: The Sequel

Remember those night sweats? Well, here's the next instalment: sleep deprivation. Your baby's sleep patterns might still be all over the place, and those hours of uninterrupted slumber might feel like a distant memory. It's hard. 18 months later I am still here. My baby slept four hours last night. I'm not going to sugarcoat this one. Don't get me wrong, you learn to operate on such little sleep which you never thought would be possible. But it is hard. That said, some of my friends had babies who slept through the night after 8 weeks (formula fed). You have no idea what type of baby you will get and it is not that you are doing something wrong. It's luck of the draw. I now whisper to my baby, 'thank you for giving me this extra time to cuddle you' as it reminds me how lucky I am to be her mama. It's important you share the rough nights with your partner. It's one thing breastfeeding a baby through the night but quite another holding a screaming baby until 3am because they're teething. Partner's step up!

Next six weeks

Self-Care, Always
Just as in the first two weeks, self-care remains paramount. Remember that you are the anchor of your family, and taking care of yourself is essential for taking care of your baby. Take those moments of respite, indulge in a warm bath when you can, and treat yourself with kindness. My baby didn't sleep much during the day so I had a little 'to-do list' when she went down, knowing it might be for 5 minutes or 60. It went like this: Water, food, bath, laundry. If I got through the first two, I'd done well.

Celebrating the Small Wins
Amid the whirlwind, take time to celebrate the small wins. Every smile, every milestone, and every moment of peace is a victory.

So here's to the next six weeks – a period of healing, bonding, and embracing the new rhythm of life. It won't always be easy, but it will always be worth it. Keep your heart open, your patience intact, and remember, you're doing an amazing job. This is the incredible adventure called motherhood!

Breastfeeding

The Awkward, Painful, and Messy Truth

Like trying to fill a moving target with a leaky hose, while both of you are still learning the instructions.

Navigating breastfeeding - it's part survival skill, part dairy farming, and a full-time job where the boss is a pint-sized milk critic.

Breastfeeding

Tender Beginnings

Breastfeeding, often envisioned as a serene and instinctive process, can start as a bittersweet journey for many new mothers. In the early days, it's not just about bonding and nourishing your newborn; it can be a time of unexpected pain and discomfort. It's about finding the right latch, the most comfortable position, and often, enduring toe-curling pain. New mothers need to know that they're not alone in this struggle and that with time, support, and sometimes medical guidance, this pain usually eases, leading to a more comfortable experience. I was amazed that as soon as my baby came out of me, she was handed to me and immediately started breastfeeding. This was incredible, I didn't know that could happen (and it doesn't happen for everyone), but after a few hours, my nipples were so sore and cracked. Start using lanolin while pregnant and use 10x a day or more in the first week the baby arrives. It's perfectly safe for the baby to ingest. Once latched, I used to count down from 10 to cope with the pain. Even the milk coming through can be painful. It feels like a tsunami coming toward the nipple. Breast milk is amazing, did you know, if your baby is cold, breast milk is warmer, if it's hot out, the milk has more water in it, if your baby is unwell, more antibodies – incredible right?

Breastfeeding

Unexpected Splashes

Picture a quiet, bonding moment during breastfeeding, and out of the blue, your baby decides it's time for a surprise milk shower. This isn't a scene from a farcical comedy; it's just another day in the life of breastfeeding. Milk somehow finds its way onto your clothes, your face, maybe the couch – it's an unpredictably messy affair. But amidst these mini milk mishaps, there's a real sense of the everyday challenges and joys of parenthood. You learn to take it in stride, armed with a burp cloth and a good-natured giggle, because this messy journey is also filled with love and unforgettable moments.

Marathon Munching

Have you heard about cluster feeding? I had no idea - imagine your baby on your boob for 24hrs! It's totally normal but really exhausting! It is a growth spurt for the baby. For me, it happened on the second night, in the sixth week and again a few months later. Partners you really have to step up during a cluster feed, it's like working a 24hr shift with no breaks. If you can provide food, water and hold the baby any opportunity then mama will survive another week!

Breastfeeding

The "Latch-on" Labyrinth

Latching – a term that becomes a central theme in your daily life, echoing in your thoughts during both sleepless nights and hectic days. Achieving that ideal latch can seem as complex and elusive as solving a Rubik's Cube with your eyes closed. Each baby is unique, presenting their style: there's the unpredictable 'frenemy latch' that's a mix of right and wrong, or the acrobatic latch that defies all the usual norms. These varied attempts at latching are part of the intricate dance of breastfeeding, a journey filled with trial, error, and eventual triumph. I went to see a latching expert at our local health centre, who was helpful. My health visitors post-birth, were lovely, however, they were early 20's and while they beautifully recited the 'new mum' textbook, for latching difficulties you need someone who has been there and done that. If you are having a lot of difficulty, then your baby could be tongue-tied. Insist on getting your baby checked as early as possible because the longer it is left the less likely you will be able to breastfeed.

Breastfeeding

Mastitis Madness

Mastitis often crashes the breastfeeding celebration, like an unwelcome visitor bringing chaos without warning. One moment, the joy of a successful feeding session fills the air, and the next, symptoms like fever, chills, and inflammation disrupt the peace. It's both alarming and discomforting when these signs abruptly appear. Imagine Rudolph's nose on your breast! During such times, it's crucial for your partner to step in, allowing you rest and recovery, particularly between feedings. Prioritising the affected breast for feeding and adding pumping sessions can help alleviate the blockage.

In an attempt to ease the discomfort, various remedies like warm and cold compresses, gentle massages, and cabbage leaves placed over the breast (not as soup!) may offer some relief. Here's a secret - your hospital will have a hospital-grade breast pump which is more powerful than something you can buy, this may provide significant relief.

Breastfeeding

Gut Health

It's imperative to be seen and thoroughly examined by a doctor before resorting to antibiotics. You don't need them unless there is an infection. Antibiotics can disrupt gut health for both you and the baby if used unnecessarily, but they might be vital if an infection is present and poses serious risks. Should antibiotics become necessary, balance your gut health with probiotics. You can try yogurt or Symprove or for a more powerful boost, I resorted to probiotics by 'Optibac' which are medically designed to protect your gut health against the destruction of antibiotics.

Breastfeeding challenges can feel isolating. My experience with healthcare providers was disheartening, as they twice resorted to prescribing antibiotics without any examination, adversely affecting both my and my baby's gut health and risking a later immunity to antibiotics. The third time mastitis hit, I insisted on seeing a doctor and he examined my breast and found there was no infection, just a blockage and no antibiotics were needed.

Breastfeeding

The 'Leaking' Surprise

Leakage: it's the unanticipated addition to your new wardrobe as a mother. Your breasts seem to have a mind of their own, choosing the most inopportune moments to let loose. Picture being in a meeting, and out of nowhere, it's as if your chest decides to host a mini fountain display. Suddenly, you find yourself amid an involuntary 'milk shower,' turning any top into a potential splash zone. It's one of those motherhood experiences that keeps you guessing and, in its unique way, reminds you of the wonders and surprises of your body's capabilities. I used pads and padded bras. If you use reusable pads, be mindful not to let your nipple sit in a wet cover because that could lead to thrush or discomfort.

Nutritional Necessities

When you're breastfeeding, your body literally takes what it needs for the baby from your body. Baby needs more calcium? It will be taken from your bones! It's an incredible way to nurture your child but stock up on your nutrition to cope with this. Breastfeeding uses 500-1000 calories, replenish this with nutritious food!

Breastfeeding

The Engorgement Extravaganza

Engorgement – it's not just a word; it's a spectacular event that turns your breasts into rock-hard, gravity-defying boulders. Your breasts become bigger, rounder, and more imposing than ever before. Even if you have lost the pregnancy pounds you may struggle to fit into your old clothes with your new double D's. A post-birth wardrobe is more about easy access for breastfeeding so think shirts and wrap tops or easy pull-down tops.

While we're talking about eyefuls, when it comes to breastfeeding in public, oddly, older women seemed to give disappointing glares more than anyone else. Men just look the other way. Young people couldn't care less.

Isn't it odd how breast enlargements are characterised around a breastfeeding woman's engorged breasts?

Breastfeeding

In the end, breastfeeding is a glorious mess of joy, pain, laughter, and tears. It's a unique journey filled with moments that make you question your sanity and moments that make you appreciate the incredible bond you share with your baby. So, embrace the hilarity, soldier through the pain, and wear those milk-stained badges with pride. You're a breastfeeding superhero, and your messy, funny, and painful adventure is uniquely yours. Cheers to the milk-spraying, nipple-twisting, and mastitis-fighting journey of motherhood!

Partner's Playbook

Welcome to the wild ride of postpartum partnership! You've been promoted to the elite squad of nappy duty, late-night lullabies, and mastering the art of one-handed snack preparation. This playbook is your secret weapon to navigate the unpredictable, yet utterly rewarding, terrain of new parenthood. Buckle up, it's going to be an unforgettable journey!

Partner's Playbook

Quick list:

1.Wash towels and bath mats twice a week or more & wash sheets twice a week and pillow case regularly

2.Laundry every day – Mum may only have a couple of Maternity pants/bras in rotation

3.Water all the time – breastfeeding is thirsty work. Consider cereal bars by the bed too

4.Empty nappy bin 3 times weekly – you'll go through 15 nappies a day

5.Empty bathroom bin daily for the first week – again it's just nice to be fresh with all the maternity pads

6.Empty normal bins – Mum should not lift anything heavy for 6 weeks

7.Meal prep – prepare finger food – think dinosaur arms

8.Hold the baby as soon as you get home to give mum a break

9.You are the 6 am duty officer! If mum has breastfed through the night then you need to let her sleep

10. Show love to your partner at every opportunity – lift her up when the hormones are dragging her down!

Partner's Playbook

Laundry Extravaganza

You'll become a laundry wizard. Expect to wash towels and bath mats twice a week, or maybe even more. Blood loss is no joke, and we want our living space to resemble a crime scene as little as possible. Also, remember to keep that washing machine running daily because Mum might only have a couple of maternity pants and bras in rotation. If you read about the night sweats then you'll understand your bed sheets should be washed twice a week and mum's pillow case daily. Don't worry this only lasts 10 days. I slept with a beach-sized towel to combat both the night sweats and the milk fountain.

Hydration Station

Water, water everywhere! Ensure there are water bottles by the bed and sofa at all times. Breastfeeding is thirsty work, and you're the designated water supplier. And while you're at it, consider stashing cereal bars by the bedside too. You'll be the midnight snack hero.

Partner's Playbook

Nappy Duty

Get ready to tackle the Everest of nappy bins. We're talking about emptying it at least three times a week because, believe it or not, we're going through a whopping 15 nappies a day. You're a nappy-changing ninja now, so embrace it. If Mama has been alone all day then she has probably changed 10+ nappies so you should try to do all nappies when you get home and at the weekends.

The Bin Brigade

The bathroom bin is your domain. Empty it daily for the first week or more. It's all about maintaining a fresh and clean environment, especially with all those maternity pads involved. Sorry for the TMI, but hey, better you know, right? Oh, and don't forget to take care of the regular bins too. New mummies should steer clear of anything heavy for six weeks. You're the heavy-lifting champion now.

Partner's Playbook

Mealtime Magic

Mums need to eat a lot to recover from birth and fuel breastfeeding. However, newborns need holding with two hands while moving around, and when seated you can move one arm but not with full movement. Prep overnight oats for Mama's breakfast and prepare finger foods if you're leaving Mum alone for any time (crudites, sandwiches, snacks etc). Think 'dinosaur arms'.

Early Morning Heroics

The 6 a.m. handover. Picture this: You, in all your glorious sleep-deprived splendour, are ready to take the torch from Mum, who has heroically breastfed through the night. Mum passes the baby to you, and in that moment, you become the Early Morning Hero. Enjoy your sunrise shift! Take the baby away from mum as soon as she finishes the morning feed and ideally head out for a walk so Mum can't hear you. I know you're tired too, but it pales in comparison to Mum's exhaustion.

Partner's Playbook

United We Parent

While your baby may not retain early memories of being held and comforted, your partner will never forget how you rose to the occasion during these demanding early days. The choice is yours: watch from the sidelines or be an unwavering pillar of support. The foundation of your partnership will be significantly shaped by the mutual support you provide each other now.

Your actions in these moments are pivotal, setting the tone for the resilience and depth of your relationship in the future. Will you be the rock she can always lean on? The sanctuary she seeks? Your child will not only witness but also feel the enduring respect and bond shared between you.

In social settings, encourage the partner who's more involved in childcare duties to share their experiences. If one partner spends the day with adults while the other craves adult interaction, when with friends, ensure the caregiving partner receives the spotlight they deserve. Publicly express your admiration and gratitude for their indispensable role, ensuring they feel valued and acknowledged.

Partner's Playbook

Cuddle King

I know after a long day of work, you are exhausted too, but it is a different kind of exhaustion. The new mama will have been holding a baby for the best part of 12 hours, she will be physically, emotionally, and mentally exhausted. If you can't come home and hold the baby for an hour with only warmth and love in your eyes, then you really need to think about what your partner has been through. On the weekends, think about giving your partner blocks of time when she can do something for herself, e.g. exercise or rest.

All the Extra Love

In between all the practical tasks, remember that your presence and support are the most precious gifts. Offer a listening ear, share the cuddles with the baby, and reassure Mum that she's doing an incredible job. You're her rock, her partner-in-crime, and her superhero. Together, you've got this!

So, gear up, partner! Your to-do list is your battle plan, and you're about to conquer the postpartum world with humour, love, and undeniable awesomeness. Welcome to the adventure of a lifetime!

Secrets After Birth

As you close this booklet and embark on your remarkable journey of parenthood, remember that you are stepping into a role filled with unparalleled love and profound transformation. Each day will bring its own set of challenges and joys, but within you lies an incredible strength and resilience. Embrace each moment, cherish the small victories, and know that you are not alone in this adventure. Your journey will be uniquely yours, a beautiful blend of laughter, tears, learning, and love. May you find joy in the chaos, strength in the struggles, and endless love in the eyes of your child. Welcome to the extraordinary world of parenthood – a journey where every step is a memory, every challenge a learning, and every moment a treasure. Here's to you, the new parent - may your heart be filled with hope, warmth, and the unending joy of discovery.

Yours,
Evelyn

Printed in Great Britain
by Amazon